Fingerprints of God

62 DAY DEVOTIONAL TO FINDING GOD IN ORDINARY CIRCUMSTANCES

Cynthia Holloway

EABooks Publishing
Your Partner In Publishing

Scripture quotations marked CSB have been taken from the Christian Standard Bible®, Copyright © 2017 by Holman Bible Publishers. Used by permission. Christian Standard Bible® and CSB® are federally registered trademarks of Holman Bible Publishers.

Scripture quotations marked (KJV), are from The Holy Bible, King James Version. The KJV is in public domain.

Scriptures marked NASB are from New American Standard Bible Copyright © 1960, 1971, 1977, 1995, 2020 by The Lockman Foundation, La Habra, Calif. All rights reserved.

Scriptures marked NIV are from THE HOLY BIBLE, NEW INTERNATIONAL VERSION®, NIV® Copyright © 1973, 1978, 1984, 2011 by Biblica, Inc.™ Used by permission. All rights reserved worldwide.

Scriptures marked NKJV taken from the New King James Version®. Copyright © 1982 by Thomas Nelson. Used by permission. All rights reserved.

Scripture quotation marked NLT are from Holy Bible, New Living Translation, copyright © 1996, 2004, 2015 by Tyndale House Foundation. Used by permission of Tyndale House Publishers, Inc., Carol Stream, Illinois 60188. All rights reserved.

Name: Cynthia Holloway
Title: Fingerprints of God: 62 Day Devotional To Finding God in Ordinary Circumstances
ISBN: hardcover - 978-1-953114-49-5
ISBN: paperback - 978-1-953114-09-9
LCCN: 2021918828

Subjects: 1 REL 012010 Religion/Christian Living/Devotional 1
2 REL 012040 Religion/Christian Living/Inspirational
3 REL 012120 Religion/Christian Living/Spiritual Growth
Interior Design by Darryl Bennett
Cover Design by Robin Black
Cover Photo Credit: iStockphoto/Saddako

Published by EA Books Publishing, a division of
Living Parables of Central Florida, Inc. a 501c3
EABooksPublishing.com

Dear Readers,

Thank you for taking the time to read and for letting God speak to you through my stories. **Fingerprints of God** *is a result of my own journaling through the years. As I prepared for this book, I read through various filled journals and became bored with my same ole thoughts pertaining to the same ole things. But, as I began to peel away my words and hurts, it was there I found God's fingerprints. He was there through all the hurt, pain, struggles, grief, and sleepless nights; God was right there all the time! God began to open my eyes to the unlimited possibilities with Him. As I began writing this book, I questioned, "From where will the inspiration come?" God told me in my spirit that He always has plenty to say and all I needed to do was be disciplined, listen, and record the experiences that He is allowing me to have with Him...fingerprints of His hand on my life. As you read, know that God has plenty to say to you as well and wants you to notice the various fingerprints He has left and will continue to leave on your life. Be ever watchful of Him working in all areas of your life. My prayer is that you will enjoy reading these words and that God will receive the glory.*

Dedication

To my Heavenly Father, I am nothing without you. Thank you for the stories and fingerprints on my life. May your words pour out of this vessel to help fill others with your love.

To my sweet Momma whom I miss terribly. All that could be counted as good within me, is a result of this strong Christian woman who now resides with her Heavenly Father. Your smile will forever be that which encourages me to keep on.

To all my mentors both old and young, thank you for your shining light and wisdom. You know who you are and my life is richer having you in my life.

To all my Sibbies who love me unconditionally, just like Jesus. You are the gift that causes my heart to overflow.

To my hubby, thank you for believing in me.

Table of Contents

Day 1
An Original

I am blessed to have four wonderful siblings in my life; they are four of the greatest gifts my mother ever gave me. One day I was catching up with one of my brothers and he shared that he had been feeling stuck in life. I asked him if there was anything he had ever wanted to do, but had not tried. After thinking for a bit, he said he always wanted to try painting. I offered him the simple advice of "well, just do it!" And you know…he did. Months later he surprised me with a beautiful painting of a pathway at sunset graced with flowers of various colors. The scene he captured was full of peace and serenity. It was his first painting ever and he wanted me to have it; his first original.

I was tearful that Thanksgiving as he presented not just me, but my mother and siblings their own original as well. Each painting depicted something uniquely significant in our life; all were masterpieces to us painted with love. That is how God sees us. Original works of art and masterpieces created with love. Each of us has been created for a specifically designed assignment while on earth. Our assignments will change throughout our lifetime but God will remain constant and has designed you uniquely for His purpose. You are a precious original, valued by God. God will reveal new talents, gifts, and abilities as you allow Him to work in your life. Consider allowing God to be the painter of your life story.

I will praise thee; for I am fearfully and wonderfully made; marvelous are thy works; and that my soul knows right well. (Psalm 139:14, KJV)

Ponder this:

What characteristics has God given you that might be used to make a positive difference in this world?

Day 2
Sing on Oh Cardinal

There he sat perched high in a tree singing his little heart out; brilliant red in color and standing out like a mighty warrior of God whose purpose was to deliver a message on this white wintery day. His melodious, inspired message reminded me that God's promises are true and we would be wise to believe them!

Some of God's messages are simple, such as, "Jesus loves you," "When you are afraid, trust Him," "Be still and know that He is God," and "Peace I give you." Ofttimes in life we tend to complicate His simple messages of love, but God's love is not complicated; we just have to learn how to accept it.

On this cold wintery morning, I accepted that God sent a cardinal my way to encourage and to deliver a simple message of love. God has sent many cardinals my way over the years and I take each sighting as a means of encouragement. I pay attention when I see or hear one and I know that God's messages deserve my full attention. Listen, for HE speaks to us through nature as well as through others. Just like the cardinal singing high in the tree, God wants to take you to higher places in your faith. Listen for His simple messages and freely embrace His love.

My sheep listen to my voice; I know them, and they follow me.
(John 10:27, NIV)

Ponder this:

What is your favorite way that God speaks to you through nature?

What other scriptures can you find that references nature and God? Reflect on the scriptures and write your thoughts.

Day 3

God's Timing

The flowers were planted with gentle love and care; neatly placed in exact order to bring a lovely arrangement of color to the rainy day…awaiting spring. We spend many hours waiting in life; waiting in traffic, waiting for results from a test, traveling, or waiting for someone or a situation to change. Life requires waiting and waiting requires patience.

Ever wonder how much time God spends waiting for us? Thankfully HE is a patient God. But it must sadden Him when we get ahead of Him and rush what is not yet meant to be. Just as the spring flowers will not survive a winter's snow, for they must wait for the sunshine and warmth to help them grow. And we too, must wait on God to make things happen in His own time. He always has a reason for what we perceive as a delay.

Consider what God might be waiting on you to do. Search your heart and listen to His voice for direction. His timing is perfect, He is never late, and He needs no reminder from us as to what time it is regarding any perceived delays. God is fully aware of where you are and where you need to be according to His will for your life.

Let all that I am wait quietly before God, for my hope is in him.
(Psalm 62:5, NLT)

Ponder this:

Reflect on a time in your life when you waited on God and witnessed his perfect timing.

Was it hard to wait on His leading? If so, how can you better wait for Him next time?

Where do you need to focus your attention regarding something that he has asked you to do? What will your plan be?

Day 4

HE Knows Your Name

Caves are interesting—dark and magical with all their wet and glistening diamonds and crystal rocks embedded in crevasses. Hidden paths await exploration by cautious feet not really sure where to step in the dark. A cave can be scary, kind of like this vast big world at times.

I visited several caves when I was younger and always felt a bit intimidated being in an enclosed dark space. But you know, even in the vast places of creation, God knows our name and knows exactly where we are at each given moment! I find it helpful to sometimes say out loud, "God knows my name!" Saying it is one thing, believing it is another, but the more you say it, the more you believe it. The more you believe it, the more you live it. The more you live it, the more you will be convinced of God and how HE protects and loves you.

The Bible says, HE even knows the number of hairs on your head (Luke 12:7). You are in the palm of God's hand, so feel His love, for HE knows you individually even in the vastness of the world. When things seem dark and overwhelming and you can't really see where to step next, trust that God is willing and able to sustain you and He will light the pathway. When things feel like they are caving in on you, trust Him, for He truly does know your name and would like nothing more than to grant your heart peace.

"I am leaving you with a gift—peace of mind and heart. And the peace I give is a gift the world cannot give, so don't be troubled or afraid."
(John 14:27, NLT)

Ponder this:

Do you trust that God knows your name?

What clear message has He given you that reinforces He knows your name?

Say "God knows my name" out loud at least three times this week.

Day 5

Clean Out the Junk

The shed is piled high with stuff I mostly find totally useless: old rakes, cans, pots, various rusty tools, outdated chairs, spiders, bugs and perhaps a mouse or two. Piles of junk are what we sometimes have in our own hearts and minds; things that are totally useless but can cause us to be filled with anxiety, depression, guilt, hate, regret, and lies. Sometimes, if we are honest, jealousy can be the root of some of these feelings and emotions. It is best to let go of those things that weigh you down, things that really do not matter in the end.

Letting go requires effort and energy but hanging on can be draining. Letting go sometimes involves forgiving others which is not always an easy thing to do. Forgiveness will lighten your heart and enable you to move forward and closer to God and that is a wonderful thing. Other people's expectations of what you should do or be could also be a contributor to some of these feelings. Draw near to God and begin to cleanse your heart of these unnecessary things. He wants to take all the stuff that drags us down in life and the negative feelings that are a result of the lies you have believed about yourself.

The enemy would like nothing more than to keep your mind and heart filled with junk. Speaking and praying out loud to God can be very freeing. And having less stuff in your heart creates more room for God!

"Create in me a clean heart, O God. Renew a loyal spirit within me."
(Psalm 51:10, NLT)

Ponder this:

What is God asking you to let go of or to cleanse from your life?

What in your life stirs up jealousy or fills your heart with anxiety?

Day 6
Simple Words

There is a young girl I mentored for 12 years; she is now an adult living a happy life. Every time I took her on an outing, whether it was to buy school supplies, get her hair cut, nails done, buy a dress for a dance, clothes shopping, trips to the zoo, museum visits, fishing, the park or a long walk, she always said, "Thank you for the day." It was such a sweet and simple sentence but one that touched me to the core of my heart. Things I normally took for granted on most days she was most grateful for.

How many times do we wake up each day or close our eyes at night and say, "Thank you God for the day?" I am sure that He, who is the giver of life and all things good, would appreciate hearing these simple words: Thank you for the day! I have made it a recent habit of walking my yard right before dusk, gazing up at the sky and right before I enter the house to close the door for the night I look up at the sky and say "Thank you, dear God, for the day." It gives closure to my day and ends it on a note of gratitude.

Perhaps tonight before you go to bed, look up at the glorious starlit sky and say a simple but heartfelt prayer thanking God for the day. After all, He is the one who gives life to enjoy. Imagine having to face life without God. I do not know about you, but I would rather not. His presence with us is the only thing we can truly count on. Gratitude goes a long way with God and our simple words of gratitude bring joy to His heart.

"So now we can rejoice in our wonderful new relationship with God because our Lord Jesus Christ has made us friends of God."
(Romans 5:1, NLT)

Ponder this:

How can you close out your day giving thanks to God?

Write a simple bedtime prayer you can remember to pray each night before closing your eyes on the day.

Write 5 things you are grateful for at the close of the day or the beginning of tomorrow.

Day 7

Stick Figures

I have a small New Testament Bible that I use for Bible studies and it is complete with stick figures to illustrate certain passages of the Bible. I love the simplicity of the figures. One of my favorites is a picture of a cross and a stick figure representing Jesus standing alone at the side of the cross. A long line forms and other stick figures are in line with bundles on their backs. As the stick figures lay their bundles down at the foot of the cross, a smile comes over each face as they lay it all at Jesus's feet. They approach the cross burdened, broken, and defeated, but once they lay it all at Jesus's feet, they are renewed and lighter. It is the same with our prayer life and coming to Jesus with all that troubles us.

Once we have given to Jesus that which troubles us, it's best to leave it there. Many times, we are tempted to pick up our bundles of troubles again, pack them neatly back in our knapsacks, and throw them right back on again. Jesus wants nothing more than for His children to be whole and He cares about every detail of our lives.

Don't spend so much time trying to "figure" things out on your own. This can lead to you becoming so overwhelmed and burdened that you no longer feel like giving it to God. By-pass the world's way of dealing with things and give it all to God first. Then be delighted, knowing He will take care of it all. Your job is to trust, believe, and carry on after you have laid it all down at His feet. Jesus already has everything about your life all "figured" out.

"Come to me all you who labor and are heavy laden
and I will give you rest.
Take my yoke upon you and learn from me,
for I am gentle and lowly in heart,
and you will find rest for your souls.
For my yoke is easy and my burden is light."
(Matthew 11:28–30, NLT)

Ponder this:

What do you need to lay at Jesus's feet?

When tempted to pick up your bundle again, what can you do instead?

Day 8

God Knows

Some days I do not feel very creative. Not sure if it has to do with the unrest in the world due to the pandemic or just my mind not knowing where to focus in these pressing times. Perhaps you are too are having similar thoughts. But God knows all about it. God knows our heart. God knows what we need. God knows what the world needs. God knows. He just knows. I can find comfort in those words. Comfort in knowing that when I fall on my knees in my closet and cover my head with my bathrobe to pray, and then just end up silent because I have no words, God knows. He understands it all. And sometimes that is all I need to know.

**"And not only so, but we glory in tribulations also;
knowing that tribulation worketh patience;
And patience, experience; and experience, hope:"
(Romans 5:3–4, KJV)**

Ponder this:

What do you know for sure about God?

Do you believe that tribulation experiences bring about hope and patience?

Day 9
Trust

Remember those spooky pictures that used to hang on your grandparent's walls and each time you walked by, the people's eyes in the photograph would follow you? How come those people never smiled I wonder?

One night as a young girl, I prepared to sleep in my grandparent's guest bedroom. I told my Papaw how scared I was to sleep in the room because of the pictures. He just laughed and then told me to repeat the following Bible verse over and over again: "What time I am afraid, I will trust in thee" (Psalm 56:3, KJV). It helped some, but as a child, I did not quite grasp the meaning that Scripture verse has for me today.

Faith is all about trust in God: trusting that HE is all–knowing and all BIG about caring for his children. I have repeated the Scripture my grandfather taught me over and over at various times in my life; it is calming and has taken hold in my heart. Faith is an ever-growing, lifelong process and I am thankful to my Papaw for planting that seed of Scripture in my heart many years ago. The next time you look at an old photograph with "moving eyes," know God watches your every movement and in him you can find peace and rest.

"Don't worry about anything; instead, pray about everything.
Tell God what you need and thank him for all he has done.
Then you will experience God's peace,
which exceeds anything we can understand.
His peace will guard your hearts and minds
as you live in Christ Jesus."
(Philippians 4:6-7, NLT)

Ponder this:

What does it mean to you knowing the eyes of God are upon you?

What was the last thing you truly trusted God with?

What do you need to trust Him with today?

Day 10

Green Beans

Picking and stringing green beans is something kids today probably do not do much of, but that was how we spent our Saturdays while growing up. It was hot, tiring, and boring work, but I think fondly of sitting in the shade with cousins, brothers, and Mamaw, talking as we strung beans until our fingers hurt. We would laugh and complain about the summer heat and looking back now, it creates a fondness in my heart for family and good conversation. Conversing with others is so important in order to build relationships. It is no different with God. He wants to be in conversation with us and be a part of our day…every day.

Based on my experience, God speaks to us through other people of faith, nature, the Bible, and in our spirits. Conversing with Him also requires listening. In fact, we would be wise to listen more and speak less when it comes to God. His word tells us to be still and know that He is God (Isaiah 46:10). Being still can be so difficult in this fast-paced world, but it is so vital to growing in Christ and learning to listen to Him.

God's messages of unconditional love are timeless and will never fade. Pay attention to the people God sends your way who are meant to encourage you along this journey of life. I am thankful for the string bean memories of my youth with my Mamaw; she never left God out of anything…even stringing beans in the hot sun with her grandchildren.

"The Lord says,
"I will guide you along the best pathway for your life.
I will advise you and watch over you."
(Psalm 32:8, NLT)

Ponder this:

Who are the people in your life who encourage you?

In what ways can you be an encourager to someone else?

Day 11
Wrapped in Love

It was the Christmas I got everything I wanted. It was also the year I learned the truth about Santa, the year my parents divorced, and the year I came to believe Jesus loved me. Life events can cause us to experience different emotions and sometimes they can be hard to control. Life can be even harder if we fail to see God in all things.

I threw all my emotions into caring for the new baby doll I got for Christmas that year. I made sure she was fed, burped, diapered, put down for naps, and wrapped in love just as any young girl excited about a new doll would do. In the midst of pain and hurt, God does the same for us…He takes care of us!

Because of God's greatest gift to us, the gift of His Son, we do not have to walk the journey of life alone. Be encouraged that God knows your name and desires to walk hand-in-hand with you during this earthly journey… caring for you each step of the way. Just as Mary wrapped her precious Jesus in swaddling clothes and just as I wrapped my baby doll, know that God wraps you up in His arms of love. Feel His presence with you for HE cares for you and every aspect of your life. Once we understand the comfort from God, we are better able to comfort others.

"And this shall be a sign unto you;
Ye shall find the babe wrapped in swaddling clothes,
lying in a manager."
(Luke 2:12, KJV)

"All praise to God the Father of our Lord Jesus Christ.
God is our merciful Father and the source of all comfort.
He comforts us in all our troubles so that we can comfort others.
When they are troubled, we will be able to give them
the same comfort God has given us."
(2 Corinthians 1:3–4, NLT)

Ponder this:

What does it mean to you to be wrapped in God's love?

$\mathcal{D}ay$ 12
Turn Around!

Sometimes God and the Holy Spirit just amaze me. Having left the drug store one day and turning down a street by our local university, I saw a person sitting on a bench and God said in my spirit, "Turn around!" "No, I'm going to my office," I said. The feeling to turn around would not let me go, so I proceeded to turn my car around three times before I finally stopped.

I was planning on getting out of my car and walking up to the person who I thought must have needed something for God to have whispered "turn around." As I pulled behind another car to park, the person on the bench was now on the move. I realized it was a woman having difficulty walking due to perhaps a disability. Just as she was crossing the street, I watched her slow and struggle a bit carrying what appeared to be a single grocery bag. Hesitantly, I pulled up beside her and asked if she needed a ride and she began making moaning sounds while looking at me; I realized she was both deaf and without speech. She understood my gesture of offering her a ride and as she entered my car, I turned up the AC as it was 85 degrees with a high humidity and we were all required to wear masks due to the COVID-19 virus. The lady pointed which way to go and she was about a mile away from her apartment. She made thank you gestures and covered her heart while maintaining eye contact as she exited my car very appreciative of my gesture. My eyes filled with tears as I was reminded that God speaks a universal language and sometimes words aren't necessary.

May we be listening always and never doubt the voice or prompting of the Holy Spirit. Sometimes we want to question whether we have truly heard from God. My advice is to just test the waters. I could have gone on my merry way to my office and ignored the so-called prompting. I trusted and was obedient; something I am not always. It has only been through trial and error that I have learned to recognize a nudging of the Spirit. Sometimes I get it wrong but I think God will always honor our attempt at doing something good for another.

"The sound of the wings of the cherubim
could be heard as far away as the outer court,
like the voice of God Almighty when He speaks."
(Ezekiel 10:5, NLT)

Ponder this:

When have you been obedient to the nudging of the Holy Spirit to do something?

How can you improve on being obedient to the voice of God?

Day 13

Squirrels

Taking a nice, long, leisurely walk can be so relaxing. I can be deep in thought about life and nature and then suddenly my dog becomes distracted and intrigued by a squirrel that he practically jerks my arm and leash off wanting to chase after it. We too can become distracted in life, stray off the path and lose focus of what God wants us to do. God is always patiently and lovingly there to help guide us back to the place of peace. It can be dangerous to stray off the path and we usually pay for our lack of focus in some form or another.

Ponder where God is leading or calling you today. Perhaps HE wants you to reach out to the less fortunate, the unemployed, the hungry, or perhaps your co-worker needs a word of encouragement. Sometimes we are striving and focused towards our own plans that we miss HIS plan totally. Calmly stop, look around and pause for a while so that you can seek His direction. Become aware of things that pull you away from Him.

The world is filled with many distractions and temptations that vie for our attention, but keeping our eyes fixed on Jesus can lead to fewer mistakes in life. We need to be ever mindful of the distracting squirrels along the pathway of life. As we observe that which is around us, we are less likely to become distracted from God's desires for us. Keeping our eyes fixed on Him can be life changing.

**"And let us run with endurance the race God has set before us.
We do this by keeping our eyes on Jesus,
the champion who initiates and perfects our faith."
(Hebrews 12:1–2, NLT)**

Ponder this:

What is your greatest temptation that keeps you off track regarding God's will for your life?

Day 14

Give Me Jesus

The world is filled with lots and lots of stuff. I know because I have lots of it! Stuff can be both a blessing and cumbersome; depends on how one looks at it, I guess. The song titled, "Give Me Jesus" is perhaps one of my most favorite songs both because of its simple melody and words that move my heart. We are wise to be thankful for all God has blessed us with. Being good stewards of all God has given is a great way to honor Him. Sharing our abundance with others bring warmth to the heart and soul. Know that one day our stuff will all turn to dust. It is what we have done with all we have been given that will matter in the end. Enjoy your stuff, but sharing it with others can bring greater joy.

"Teach those who are rich in this world not to be proud
and not to trust in their money, which is so unreliable.
Their trust should be in God,
who richly gives us all we need for our enjoyment.
Tell them to use their money to do good.
They should be rich in good works
and generous to those in need,
always being ready to share with others."
(1 Timothy 6:17–18, NLT)

Ponder this:

When did you last give something away?

Could you this day donate something of value to some organization?

Day 15
Fences

For the first time in my life, I am considering putting a big fence around the property of my home. The deer are giving my dog a fit and while I love nature, I have to consider the safety and sanity of my pet. He gets bent out of shape with frustration because he cannot chase the deer that wander majestically into his space.

While fences can serve a purpose in life, they sometimes can be misused, such as building fences around our hearts when we become wounded by someone we trusted or loved. God wants to heal your hurt and pain and He will help you to break down the barriers you have created in your life. We have to use discernment as to when we need to establish boundaries but to totally fence yourself in can lead to a lonely life.

Life is meant to be shared and enjoyed. God designed us to crave love and interaction with others. I encourage you to start learning to trust others and know that perhaps your life can open up to endless possibilities of friendship and love. Give God your heart and hurt. Begin today to take down the fence one piece at a time. Test the waters and see where trusting in God will lead you. You just might find a pleasant surprise of joy in abundance awaiting you. His divine protection is all you need and He is the healer of all hurt.

"For He will conceal me there when troubles come;
He will hide me in His sanctuary.
He will place me out of reach on a high rock."
(Psalm 27:5, NLT)

Ponder this:

Where have you build emotional fences within your life?

Is there someone you need to forgive and to open your heart to God's healing?

Ask God to begin healing your heart of any pain associated with past hurts.

Day 16
Reflections

As I sit at my computer typing this devotion, I see the reflection in my computer screen of the majestic stature of the pine trees stretching up towards heaven and the maples with leaves on their branches like tiny gloves in the cold January weather. These trees are all they were created to be. They remind me to be all I was created to be, today, in this moment, or later in the day when perhaps my routine is interrupted or gotten off course. We are all meant to be a reflection of Christ…today, tomorrow and forevermore.

Whatever comes my way, I hope I can reflect on this moment of seeing the trees showing their beauty, their strength and their peace no matter what the weather. May it be so with you today as well! Peace, beauty and purpose: We all have it. As you go and do something good with it, know your actions are a reflection of Him. The more time we spend with Christ, the more we will be a reflection of Him.

Being a reflection of Christ requires kindness, gentleness, self-control, faithfulness, joy, peace, patience, goodness and love. These characteristics are all what the Bible call Fruits of the Spirit (Galatians 5:22–23, NIV). Someone once said, we may be the only Jesus other people see. Let God's light reflect upon you so that you may be a constant reflection of Him.

**"But each day the Lord pours His unfailing love upon me,
and through each night I sing His songs,
praying to God who gives me life."
(Psalm 42:8, NLT)**

Ponder this:

What fruit of the spirit gift can you most identify with?

Spend some time reading Galatians 5:22–23 and ponder which ones you need to further develop. How will you do this?

Day 17
Get Behind Me satan!
(small s on purpose)

I found an old letter from 1995 today that my mother had written (typed) to me. It was a time in my life when I was a bit down for various reasons: I found out I could not have children, and my father had decided he no longer wanted anything to do with me and I was depressed.

Mom knew what I was going through and one day I received a letter in the mail with her advice. She wrote, "Sometimes I feel like I am so incompetent to help my children when they are having a difficult time understanding things that come their way. Sometimes we get confused listening to other people that we forget that God is our closest friend. He's been and felt all that we feel and when you get so down and out, just talk to Him out loud and tell the devil to leave you alone. You may have to do this a lot of times even in a day, but trials hit and then JOY. Don't put all your faith in your therapist; he can help you some, but God is the one doing the work. Just keep using your talents every opportunity you get, and you will be shown the job you are to do. The devil is trying to get you discouraged so you won't have the energy to serve the Lord, and when the devil has us where he wants us, he doesn't bother us anymore, but when you try to serve God, he is always around, so just tell the devil to 'Get thee behind me satan!'"

Momma went on to write, "I want you to know I love you and I pray you will find peace, good health and happiness and you will if you trust in God and stop worrying over things you don't understand. I love you… always Mom."

Twenty-three years later…mom still had the best advice; wish she were still here so I could tell her, but she is with Jesus now who always has the best advice for life. Momma knew Jesus had the best advice left behind for us in Scripture and she just passed on to me all she had learned from God her Creator.

The letter is now beautifully framed and I cherish her wise and profound words to this day. She left a legacy that her children follow closely. Sometimes in life, we have to command the enemy to "get behind me!" Jesus even told the enemy to get behind Him and I personally give no credit to the enemy whatsoever in my life and that's why I use a small s when referring to him. I know God is the ruler over all, and we do not have to bow to life's challenges or hurts for we can claim victory through Christ. The enemy has no power over you!

"The name of the Lord is a strong fortress;
the godly run to Him and are safe."
(Proverbs 18:10, NLT)

Ponder this:

Where do you feel most vulnerable or challenged regarding the enemy?

Do you fully accept that God has won the power over the enemy in this world? Celebrate this victory within you!

Day 18
Amazing Grace

"Amazing grace, how sweet the sound that saved a wretch like me...." We are all familiar with the words of *Amazing Grace*.[1] But apart from the song, are you truly aware of God's Amazing Grace?

Look around you, His grace is everywhere. See Him in the beauty of a sunrise and see Him in the colors of fall and spring. Feel His grace in the cold arctic air of winter and accept His grace as He forgives us of all trespasses. Thank Him for the grace He shows every day. We are not perfect and each day comes with its own challenges, but because of God's grace, we shall prevail.

You may feel undeserving of His grace, but that is what makes it so beautiful. A gift is meant for enjoyment and fulfillment, and that is what God's gift of grace is to us. We were put on this earth to share about His grace with others, so do not be afraid to let your light shine for Him. Grace, it truly is amazing...and when "we've been there ten thousand years," it will still be amazing.

---

[1] John Newton, *The First Christian Hymnal* (Grand Rapids, MI: William B. Eerdmans Pub. Co., 1929), 136.

"And since it is through God's kindness,
then it is not by their good works. For in that case, God's
grace would not be what it really is – free and underserved."
(Romans 11:6, NLT)

Ponder this:

Look for evidence of God's grace in your life; where do you see it most today?

Day 19
Life's Journey

I remember a song my parents use to sing when I was growing up titled, *I Wouldn't Take Nothing for My Journey Now*. I used to sing that song as I was doing my chores; I found the words to be both calming and inspirational and the song helped to keep my mind off the tasks at hand.

Though the journey in life may seem long and laborious at times, it truly is short and fast-paced and filled with unexpected surprises, challenges, laughter and struggles. Life is a journey and one small stepping stone often leads to a bigger plan and place. It is important that we do not rush the process.

Often with clients, I have used the analogy of a stream with stepping stones. People often want to jump from one big stone to the next missing the smaller stones in between. We often have to pause, catch our breath and rest before we move on and the smaller stones represent that. We must remain focused on our larger goals while at the same time enjoying the journey of getting there. So, go for it.

If God has placed a desire in your heart, stop putting it off. Know that the journey is so much sweeter with Him. May you feel His presence with you as you begin this remarkable new adventure!

**"The LORD gives His people strength.
The LORD blesses them with peace."
(Psalm 29:11, NLT)**

Ponder this:

What new adventure is God calling you to experience?

Day 20
More Than Amazed

More than amazed…that is what I am feeling this day. I just listened to a song that caused my heart to stir and appreciate all the blessings we are given on a daily basis. Music can be very therapeutic and the benefits of a good song can last all day. Music has served as a therapeutic tool throughout my lifetime. I love a good old gospel song and even rock and roll while riding in my car; both can be energizing!

It truly is amazing what we as individuals are able to accomplish throughout the day. We can wear ourselves out on any given day. God does not want us frantic, but He does not want us wasting time away either. Rejoice that you have the abilities and all that you might need to lend a helping hand to someone God has placed in your pathway. God appreciates your endeavors and He is counting on you to continue the work of His kingdom here on earth.

Perhaps you are going through a difficult time right now. I encourage you to put on some good music…something that speaks to your soul. God wants you to remain encouraged and to be thankful in spite of challenges you may have to face in this life. If you are feeling lost, know that He will find you. Listen, for He is calling your name…now isn't that amazing?!

"The Lord replied to Moses,
"I will indeed do what you have asked,
for I look favorably on you,
and I know you by name."
(Exodus 33:17, NLT)

Ponder this:

Do you truly believe that God has a purpose for your life?

How has God revealed His purpose for your life?

What is your favorite uplifting song? Put it on your playlist so you can listen to it often.

Day 21
The Shining Christmas Tree

The silver tree shone brightly as the color wheel teased the branches with a rainbow of colors. Huge satin red balls hung on the tree like red delicious apples. My grandparents always decorated their tree the same every Christmas. As a child that was the most beautiful tree symbolizing love, hope and peace.

For me now, the shining tree represented the light of Christ known to shine through us. The red balls represented the blood He shed and the color wheel represented the beautiful changes God can make in our lives. I never knew there was such a thing as a "live" Christmas tree while growing up. I thought everyone had aluminum trees with color wheels! At an early age I did know, however, that God was the answer to all of life's problems. God doesn't always make the problems go away, but He makes handling problems a lot easier.

I often wonder where that old aluminum tree ended up, but I don't need it to be reminded of God's love for me. I'm reminded of that every day. Just look around you and you will be, too! Remember that Christ is the real reason for Christmas and His love is a shining gift to the whole world!

"Greater is he that is in you than he that is in the world."
(1 John 4:4, KJV)

Ponder this:

What is your favorite Christmas memory?

How can that favorite Christmas memory help you throughout the year?

Was the Christmas story read to you as a child?

When did you last read the Christmas story found in the gospel of Luke 2:1–21?

Day 22
When God Nudges

Ever wonder why we get those little feelings in our spirit about something or someone? They are to be paid attention to. Perhaps you have gotten someone on your mind only to find out a day or two later that that person had been going through something significant. The feeling you had previously was God's way of nudging you to pray for that person or to reach out to them. The Holy Spirit often has us intervene on behalf of others. Perhaps you could send a card, call the person, or just stop and pray.

When God puts someone on your heart, be obedient and follow through; do not ignore the feeling. You will get better at it the more you trust the feeling. The best thing that comes from this is, people get to see the miracle of Jesus and you get to witness God at work. That in itself is a true miracle and something God wants us as believers to experience.

God is alive and shows His love for believers through random acts of service and kindness. I have witnessed His mighty work over and over again, and if you have been walking with the Lord long enough and in His obedience then I know you have too. If not, just believe and ask Him to use you to be the miracle that someone else might just need. You can start today!

**"And grieve not the holy Spirit of God,
whereby ye are sealed unto the day of redemption."
(Ephesians 4:30, KJV)**

Ponder this:

Has God placed someone on your heart today that you need to call or send a message of encouragement to?

Have you ever been the one who needed the encouragement and received a phone call or card that same day? If so, reflect on how that made you feel in the moment.

How can you better understand the prompting of the Holy Spirit?

Day 23
The Unexpected

We never know what God has in store for us from day to day and that can be exciting if you like change. Most people tend to not like change, but others thrive on adventure and the unexpected. Sometimes God has a way of shaking us up unexpectedly.

Case in point, one morning my husband and I were leaving the house to run errands; we were detained a bit because my husband had left his cell phone in the house. As we were pulling out of the driveway, I witnessed our neighbor flip off the top steps of his home landing face down on his sidewalk. I took off running towards him as my husband called 911. I went to my neighbor who was breathing and barely conscious; I assured him he was not alone and help was on the way. I could not see his face but I knew he was badly injured. EMTs finally arrived, and my neighbor succumbed to his injuries later that night. His wife and boys were distraught and I was the person they were looking to for final closure since I had seen what happened.

I have no idea why God chose me to be the person who witnessed his fatal fall, but all I can do is point back to God when speaking with this family and assure them that their loved one was never alone in his fatal fall. EMT's took very good care of him. I relayed to the family that I thought God had spared them having to see their dad and husband in this tormented state; the family had gone out to run errands and he had gone to check the mail before experiencing his fatality.

If my husband had not left his phone in the house which delayed us by a few minutes, we perhaps would not have witnessed the falling. God knew the man needed someone with him during his final hours and with help coming quickly, it perhaps allowed the family the time to get to the hospital and say goodbye before disconnecting the ventilator.

We never know how God might use us from one minute to the next. Be open to His leading and watch Him work through you. Know that one interruption for you might just be God working in someone else's life.

**"But Martha was pulled away by all she had to do in the kitchen.
Later, she stepped in interrupting them.
"Master, don't you care that my sister
has abandoned the kitchen to me?
Tell her to lend me a hand."
Jesus answered and said to her, "Martha, Martha,
you are worried and troubled About many things.
But one thing is needed, and Mary has chosen that good part,
which will not be taken away from her."
(Luke 10:40–42 NKJV)**

Ponder this:

Think of various times when your life has been interrupted. Can you see the hand of God in that particular situation?

Day 24
Restless

Sometimes life seems restless. We just plug along day after day and not much happens in the way of excitement. It is important to use this time to rest, take care of your body, refocus, and re-establish, because it usually means God is preparing you for something. Restlessness is a part of life. We may not like it and it is important during these times that we strive to stay uplifted, supported, and energized.

Sometimes we might even have to change up our routine a bit. Routine, I think, can lead to boredom which often then leads to unhealthy means of keeping life interesting. Overspending, overindulging, sleeping too much, becoming lackluster, not fulfilling obligations, and lack of follow through with projects are often signs of boredom. Be careful during this time of restlessness to keep your spirits up, stay connected to God, know that He is working, and appreciate this time of rest He has given you so you can be your best when God makes it clear which direction you are to follow. Trust He is working even when you are feeling restless.

**"He who heeds the word wisely will find good,
and whoever trusts in the Lord, happy is he."
(Proverbs 16:20, NKJV)**

Ponder this:

What do you do when feeling restless?

Is this behavior healthy or unhealthy?

How can you make healthier choices? Ask God to help you.

Day 25
Change Your View

This morning as I walked downstairs, a particular chair in the corner of my living room looked so inviting. The sun shone brightly through the windows and it was as if the chair had called my name to come sit awhile, and you know, I did. I usually take my quiet time in another room, in another chair but this morning I moved my devotional things and Bible and placed them on a table by the chair in this new place. As I sat down, I noticed my two windows with the sun streaming in and I could see my neighbor's beautiful red maple, azaleas, dogwoods, and all the glories of springtime. My mood was suddenly lightened as I observed a neighbor working in his yard. My view had changed and so had my perspective and mental attitude.

We are in the middle of a virus pandemic: COVID–19. It has restricted people to their homes and only allowed us to go out to stores for essential reasons. People are dying and the world is changing. God says to "fear not" … even in the middle of a pandemic. Sometimes we have to move our chair to have a better view and outlook which helps us be grateful for the beauty that surrounds us. It doesn't mean we are in denial of all that is happening around us. It's just that we are keeping our eyes on our creator.

God gives us His beauty in many forms so we might have peace; all we have to do is pay attention. Because of God's grace in abundance, we can move forward through it all, and in times of uncertainty. God will often rearrange things in our lives that are necessary, but we can trust Him. The view and outlook of life can be so much better with Him. Journey with Him today.

**"And the God of all grace will himself restore you
and make you strong, firm and steadfast."
(1 Peter 5:10, NIV)**

Ponder this:

Where in your life do you see God's hand attempting to rearrange things in your life?

Are you reluctant to let go and let Him change your view?

Consider this day moving your chair; read your devotion in a new place and see if your perspective changes.

Day 26

A Sweet-Smelling Savior

This morning I dropped a whole bottle of my favorite perfume on my bathroom floor causing it to smash into many small pieces. Fragrant liquid and shards of glass were all over my bathroom. Just the day before, my husband had commented how much he liked the smell of the perfume on me; I had been wearing it for years.

While down on my knees cleaning up the mess, I was reminded by God that He is a sweet-smelling fragrance and if I "put Him on every day," then I really have no need for perfume. I smiled at this thought and said in my heart, "Yes, this is so true." Perfume is nice; I love it. But the real message for me that morning was "Just put-on Jesus!" He is the fragrance we all need.

By the way, the name of the perfume was Happy! Be happy in the Lord today for He needs you smelling like Him so others will be attracted to His grace and mercy.

"And walk in love, as Christ also hath loved us,
and hath given himself for us an offering and a sacrifice to God
for a sweet smelling savour."
(Ephesians 5:2, KJV)

Ponder this:

What small gesture of kindness could you extend to someone today?

Day 27
A Radiant Light

Are you plugged in? I mean really plugged in so that the light of Christ is shining in you? We are called to be the light to a dark world. It really isn't possible to be a light to the whole world, but our world could consist of the people we come in contact with on a daily basis. Our world is the place God has us at any given moment of time. Could be the clerk we are purchasing coffee from or the person we are standing behind in the checkout line. It doesn't matter where we are, we can be a light shining for Christ.

Being plugged in to Christ is vital. Just like a lamp has to be plugged in to electricity to be of any use, we must be plugged into Christ on a daily basis. Just like the switch on a lamp is turned on and off in order for it to be illuminated again it must be plugged in.

Bible study, prayer, fellowship with other believers, talking with family and friends about God's goodness are all ways of being plugged in. Don't lose your light, for God has called you to be His shining example using the gifts He has given you. Sometimes a smile goes a long way in making a difference in someone else's life and I've heard that a smile uses less muscles than frowning so that's good for facial wrinkles! Put on the light of Christ today and know that you are possibly illuminating the pathway of someone who has lost their way.

"For God, who said, "Let light shine out of darkness,"
made His light shine in our hearts
so we could know the glory of God
that is seen in the face of Jesus Christ."
(2 Corinthians 4:6, NIV)

"If then your whole body is full of light,
having no part dark,
the whole body will be full of light,
as when the bright shining of a lamp gives you light."
(Luke 11:36, NKJV)

Ponder this:

How can you reflect the light of Christ to someone else today?

Consider the ways you are plugged in to Christ. Are you consistent in maintaining your light?

Cynthia Holloway

Day 28

Red Rover Red Rover

Driving into my office this morning, I happened to notice about ten red rose bushes on someone's property; they were magnificent. My Momma had pretty roses too at the last place she lived; full, radiant, red bushes and she took pride in comparing my tiny buds with hers.

When I saw the red roses today, I remembered a game I played as a little girl on Sunday evenings and sometimes during school. The game consisted of boys and girls lining up on two sides and calling someone from the opposite side to "come on over!" The idea was for the person coming over, to break through the other team as they held hands forming a tight line. If you broke through then you got to take one of their team members, and if you did not break through, you were then part of the other team. Before a name was called the team would say, "red rover, red rover, send (so and so) right over!" It was a fun game and I always got excited when my name was called. Thankfully, with God, we do not have to choose sides, break barriers, or wait for Him to approve us acceptable. He is always there calling our name, wanting to do for us. And He always accepts us just as we are.

Are you able to discern His voice amongst the noise of daily life? Be mindful of what He is saying and don't forget to stop and smell the roses along the way!

"I am the rose of Sharon, and the lily of the valleys."
(Song of Solomon 2:1, KJV)

Ponder this:

Listen closely, is God calling your name today?

Have you been obedient or reluctant to do as He has asked of you?

Day 29
Lint Roller

I love a good lint roller; just something about rolling it over your clothes and cleaning off all the little white specks that seem to just magnetize themselves to dark clothing including dog hair! Thank God for small inventions. Cleaning oneself up takes effort sometimes but thank God we do not have to be totally clean before we can come to Him; He takes us, lint and all!

Our sins stick to God and He discards them to exist no more. Sounds pretty incredible and easy, doesn't it? Just like operating a lint roller; roll it over ourselves and the specks are gone! God is so good to provide His son to redeem us from our sins and all the specks that are noticeable to others. He does not judge us and never fails to keep us spotless before Him. Only by His grace do we have this gift!

Next time you use a lint roller, remember that God wipes away all specks and ugly spots in our lives and cleanses us from all unrighteousness. His gift of forgiveness to you is timeless, practical, and of utmost value. Be grateful to a risen Savior who always forgives even the darkest of stains in our lives.

**"If we confess our sins, he is faithful and just
and will forgive us our sins
and purify us from all unrighteousness."
(1 John 1:9, NIV)**

Ponder this:

What sins are you having a hard time letting go?

Do you believe Jesus has forgiven each one? Trust that His word is true and that you are truly forgiven. Memorize the above scripture.

Purchase a small lint roller and keep it in sight to remind you of God's lint-removing power over your life.

Day 30

Lost, Stuck and Found

Because my dog Grason walks around with a ball in his mouth all the time, I am constantly playing ball with him. Often, he gets one of his many balls stuck under a piece of furniture and becomes upset, barking and letting me know of his dilemma. It does not matter that he has ten other balls in his toy basket…he wants the one he has been playing with and none of the other ones will do.

As I struggled to get down on my hands and knees the other day and retrieve his ball from under the furniture, it got me to thinking about having it all and still going after the one that got away. Reminds me of the Bible story of God going back for the one lost sheep. God loves us so much that He will pursue us, find us and shepherd us as one of His own. Similar as to how my dog Grason treats his play ball, like it is the only one and nothing will satisfy him unless he rescues the one that is lost.

I want you to know that you are not lost my friend if you know Christ. God knows right where you are at any given moment. You might feel stuck and unable to get out from under the current burden you are feeling, but rest assured, God passionately cares about what you are going through. Sometimes all you have to do is just roll to Him with your problems and allow Him to rescue you out from under that burden which has caused you to feel frustrated or sad.

God will constantly pursue you and He will not leave you stuck, lost or forgotten. Be quick to bounce back to Him and He will rescue you from all troubles.

**"As a shepherd looks after his scattered flock when he is with them,
so will I look after my sheep.
I will rescue them from all the places
where they were scattered on a day of clouds and darkness."
(Ezekiel 34:12, NIV)**

Ponder this:

What could you turn over to God fully this day?

What is weighing heavy on your heart today? Will you give it to God or keep allowing it to weigh you down?

Day 31
Appreciate

Ofttimes in life we start taking things for granted. I was toweling off my fur baby after a walk in the pouring rain and I saw how much he appreciated it. Prior to us adopting him, he was a street dog found roaming around in South Carolina. I think he appreciates everything. Based on his former life, he realizes how different his life is now and his tail wags so much we call him Wiggle Butt. He was patient and kind while I worked diligently to dry him off. Something that was laborious and time consuming to me was almost a reward to him.

How many times do we take the mundane occurrences in life and turn them into joyous occasions? Grab joy when you can, seize the opportunities directly in front of you, appreciate where you are at this given moment in your life and laugh even when it's wet outside.

There is true joy to be found in the journey as long as we are walking with God. Being grateful even for the rainy seasons of our life can be hard to do but your attitude is everything sometimes. Trust that joy is coming and learn to appreciate all that is before you and be grateful this day. Don't be afraid to splash through a mud puddle or take a walk in the rain without an umbrella. Just be sure to towel-off later!

"I will send you rain in its season, and the ground will yield its crops and the trees their fruit."
(Leviticus 26:4, NIV)

Ponder this:

Are you in a rainy season of life or a harvest season?

What light-hearted thing could you do today that would bring your heart joy?

What makes you joyful? What makes you happy?

How are joy and happiness different?

Day 32
Momma Said

Speaking previously about walking in the rain; my Momma said to always do that. She was one who loved to walk in the rain without an umbrella. I have a picture of her sitting on my sister's deck before she died having a drink with a fancy straw, wearing a pair of summer shorts and holding a duck handled bright yellow umbrella. At that point in her life, her health was declining and holding the umbrella was her way of being fun-loving! What a trooper she was through it all. Momma was also one who allowed my siblings and I to play in the rain in our bathing suits; I mean the pouring down rain. I have such sweet memories of splashing in the mud puddles without a care in the world. It is one of the fondest memories I have of my Momma and the rain.

Jesus supplies the rain in our life and times of sunshine. He provides all things but sometimes, we go through seasons of draught. Times when we feel dry, unproductive or stale. Trust that God is at work even in those times. He knows what season we need to be in and sometimes He just wants us to relax and trust that a time of refreshing rain is coming. Rain that will restore, refresh and replenish all that has been damaged throughout life.

I've just looked at the weather for tomorrow and it's supposed to rain. Looks like I'll be walking without my umbrella and thinking of my Momma and all she said while on earth. It will be a guaranteed bad hair day and the forecast will be a bit dreary, but God's promises remind us that showers of blessings are coming!

**"The LORD will open the heavens,
the storehouse of his bounty,
to send rain on your land in season
and to bless all the work of your hands.
You will lend to many nations but will borrow from none."
(Deuteronomy, 28:12, NIV)**

Ponder this:

When was the last time you walked in the rain?

Where in your life do you need God's showers of blessings?

How will you enjoy the rainy season of your life?

Day 33
Where is the Joy?

We all want mountain top experiences in life. Unfortunately, when they come, we wish we could stay there but we know in our heart it's unrealistic. Life happens. After my mom died, I had a very hard time finding my joy. Nothing prepared me for not being able to put my arms around her or feel her touch again. We have all had various losses in life and if you haven't then you will.

My one word of focus over the year after she died was *joy*. I was grieving and needed to journey through this life changing event. I know the "joy of the Lord is my strength" and I clung to that verse in the midst of my grief. But somedays I was just rolling out of bed without feeling like doing so. I also know there is joy all around us even in the midst of life's events. God knows our hearts and desires for us to have joy and total joy is found through Him. When we focus on Him and His perfect plan for our lives then we can be better prepared for the journey. It does not mean that experiencing a loss will be easy, and there is no timeframe regarding when we will feel back to ourselves. But we can depend on Jesus to be with us.

If you are grieving a loss of any kind today, trust that your Heavenly Father sees you and knows your pain. Be patient with yourself, for joy can be found again. I encourage you to seek professional help with either a counselor or doctor if you feel stuck. Grief is a voyage that no one can take for you, and if we are fortunate enough to have loved in this life, then we will experience loss. Invite God to travel with you and know that He always restores that which has been taken, even joy.

**"Nehemiah said, "Go and enjoy choice food and sweet drinks,
and send some to those who have nothing prepared.
This day is holy to our Lord. Do not grieve,
for the joy of the Lord is your strength."
(Nehemiah 8:10, NIV)**

Ponder this:

Have you ever experienced loss of joy?

Did you also experience God's restoration of that which was lost?

Write 5 things you are grateful for this day as a way of helping to restore
your joy. Continue this practice as often as you can.

Day 34
The Voice of God

I was having trouble sleeping last night and was awake throughout the night. Nothing really on my mind but I starting reliving the day; some of you will understand that. Just as I was beating myself up for something I said or did, God's thought came to me and said in my spirit, "When you come to me, you should always feel better, not worse after having spent time with me." Wow, that got my attention and was so very freeing and got me to thinking that God is not a voice of criticism, defeat, down casting, chastisement, or discouragement.

Sometimes we get stuck in life by listening to the wrong voices. God says to "bring all our cares to Him." That includes our tendencies to beat ourselves up over something we should not have done or said. God is a God of kindness, forgiveness and gentleness. Yes, He does have to correct us sometimes but never in a condescending voice or one that criticizes.

Bring your thoughts to God and leave them there trusting Him; you should feel better by doing so and if not, perhaps you are listening to the wrong voice. We would be wise to get out of our own head and get on the same page as God. Remember, if we ask him, he forgives all our sins, and that includes our thoughts. Listen to His quiet voice giving you peace and reassurance.

**"And we have come to know and to believe
the love that God has for us.
God is love, and the one who remains in love
remains in God, and God remains in him."
(1 John 4:16, CSB)**

Ponder this:

Do you have healthy means of coping with sleepless nights? If not, what could you improve on?

Have you been obedient to the voice of God? What is He asking of you? Begin to explore and journal your thoughts.

Day 35
All That I Have

Reflecting on the day as I was about to fall asleep one night, I was overwhelmed by all that God has given and blessed me with. Everything I have belongs to Him and is a result of His goodness. It is overwhelming at times and takes energy to maintain it all, but God gives me the energy and organization skills needed and a supply of resources that only comes from Him. I am talking about material stuff… like most people have. I feel so underserving sometimes and feel compelled to use it to help and bless others if I can; this keeps my heart at peace. Whether it's opening my home to house a visitor, family or friend, or using my stuff to entertain and bring joy into someone else's life; it is all to be used for His glory. Sometimes guilt comes from having so much and I do not understand it all, but I am learning that this is the life God has given me and it must be used for Him. I love to give stuff away and watch how it makes someone else happy. Not everyone is called to do this but it works for me at this time in my life. We must all give account someday of how we have lived our life and what we have to show with our talents. It is never too late to begin anew. Never lose sight of all things being from God!

> **"But it was your own eyes that saw all**
> **these great things the LORD has done."**
> **(Deuteronomy 11:7, NIV)**

Ponder this:

What has God blessed you with and how can you use it to bring glory to
Him?

Day 36
Chewing Gum

During a road trip to North Carolina to see my family, I stopped at a restaurant for a little break. I had been traveling a little over four hours and my mind was calling for a cup of hot tea and relaxation. As I drove up to the front of the restaurant, I noticed a man sitting on a bench. As soon as I stopped my car, I had a nudging thought to give the man a pack of chewing gum I had put in my purse that morning before leaving the house. Give the man my chewing gum? Why would I think that? I thought the nudging to be rather strange, but I am learning that those "ideas" from God sometimes do not make sense at the time.

As I made my way into the restaurant, I promised I would offer the gum if the man was still there upon my leaving. Sure enough, he was. "Give him the pack of gum and some money," came a thought that I know was God speaking to my heart. I spoke to the man and learned he was traveling around on foot. I noticed a small bundle of personal belongings next to him and as he spoke, I also noticed he had no front teeth! None! "God," I said in my heart, "How can I offer a pack of gum to a man with no teeth?" It made no sense to me, but I did it. The man sincerely thanked me and dug into his small bundle and produced an old book that he said someone had given to him. It was grimy and stained; a religious book of some sort.

He said as I gave him the pack of gum and money, "As you can see, I have no teeth for chewing gum but this gum allows for me to be able to give something to someone else, and for that I am grateful." My heart was moved. A pack of gum that for me was a road trip treat, to be chewed and tossed out now had become a valuable prize that a homeless man could use to thank someone else.

I kept that old stained book as a reminder of a person giving all he had in the moment to a total stranger. Kind of like how Jesus is, except He gave His life as a ransom for all. All He asks in return is to receive His gift, believe in Him and share His love with others. Do your best this day, this week, this time in your life to embrace the love of Jesus and to share His gift in whatever way He has called you to do so. God can use anything we have as a means of ministering.

> **"And let us not grow weary while doing good,**
> **for in due season we shall reap if we do not lose heart.**
> **Therefore, as we have opportunity, let us do good to all,**
> **especially to those who are of the household of faith."**
> **(Galatians 6:9–10, NKJV)**

Ponder this:

Have you ever been the recipient of a random act of kindness?

Reflect back on a conversation with a total stranger. What did you offer in the way of encouragement to that person? Could you reach out to someone today? Will you?

Day 37
Bumpy Times

Our church was doing a one-word study for the year and I chose the word joyful as my word to reflect, meditate, ponder, experience, and seek out for the year. I found some wonderful scriptures to meditate and focus on and God recalled scripture to me that I needed to see in a new light. Joyful does not necessarily mean that I need more joy; however, I welcome that. But it was more about needing to feel and appreciate joy.

Sometimes we get so down in life focusing on the wrong things that we fail to really appreciate all that is going on around us. How wonderful that God allows goodness at the same time of experiencing sorrow. Losing my Momma was probably the hardest thing I have ever experienced in my life regarding loss. I will never be the same but that is not necessarily a bad thing. Through the journey of grief, I became more aware of God's ever-abiding presence and God has given me the time to reflect and grieve. Thank you, God!

Joy, or finding joy, can be eye-opening if we know how to look for it. We may see it and feel it, but then we have to appreciate it. Right now, as I write this, I am 37,000 feet in the air and it is a little bumpy. I have experienced bumpy times in my life. Events that left me scared, lonely, anxious, sad, and a bit uncertain. Right now, I can choose to focus on the bumpiness of the skies or focus on the great week I have had in the glorious sunshine with palm trees and gorgeous water-colored skies. I can appreciate that we are able to afford travel, have excellent health, and can share all that we have with others at times. Thank you, God, that there is and can be joy in the journey no matter what our life destination may be.

"Shout with joy to the Lord, all the earth!
Worship the Lord with gladness.
Come before him, singing with joy."
(Psalm 100:1, NLT)

Ponder this:

What was the last bumpy ride in life you experienced with God?

In what ways can you improve on allowing God to be the pilot of your life?

Day 38
Turtles on a Log

What a glorious day it is: on my bike this Father's Day peddling away thoughts of my earthly father with whom I have not had a relationship with for over forty years. God has healed my heart and dried my tears but I still think about him each Father's Day. As I write this, I am seated on a bench with a warm summer breeze tickling my skin and a view of a small lake in front of me surrounding a golf course. While I peddled my way to this favorite spot, I passed another small body of water and saw four young turtles sunning themselves on a log. They were all shiny and slick from the water as the sun reflected off their shells. Kindly, they allowed me one quick photo before plopping themselves back into the water. Such a sweet scene, briefly captured only because I was looking in the right direction.

God gives us little bursts of peace throughout life. They are meant to inspire, settle, encourage, and cause us to glorify in Him. Life is a moment-by-moment experience with many God moments along the way. Sometimes it might feel like we are turtles slowly climbing to higher ground. But just as soon as we think that, God lifts us up with His amazing power. We slip and slide through life at times but God is always at work. Be on the lookout for His surprises. His peace offerings are in abundance. Thanks be to God!

**"Peace I leave with you; my peace I give you.
I do not give to you as the world gives.
Do not let your hearts be troubled
and do not be afraid."
(John 14:27, NLT)**

Ponder this:

Take a walk or bike ride and observe God at work through nature.

How does observing nature encourage your heart?

Day 39
Seashells

When I was growing up, I loved Show and Tell in school. One Show and Tell day, I decided to talk about my seashell collection. As a young girl of ten years old, I had visited the beach only one time, so I was very proud of my seashell collection. As I excitedly shared about my collection of shells, one of my classmates started laughing hysterically and blurted out that I was saying "she shells" not "seashells." I was saying "she shells" but I honestly did not know I was using the wrong word. I was really embarrassed and quickly sat down. I have no recollection as to whatever became of that seashell collection and I do not recall having any further interest in collecting shells as a child.

My life experiences since then have allowed me to visit many beautiful beaches throughout my travels. I never one time brought home any shells from these great beaches, but one day while traveling I was walking along a parking lot and noticed a small shell at my feet. I never gave it much thought and just stepped over the shell but I suddenly felt the urge to pick it up and put it in my pocket. I thought a parking lot was a strange place for a seashell. For a few days, the little shell rested on my hotel vanity but eventually ended up tossed in my suitcase. On this particular trip, I had to be away from home for two weeks and every day or so I would find a shell. The shell became a sign of encouragement for me, assuring me that God was in the midst of my circumstances. I never purposely went on a hunt for shells; they just showed up sometimes in unusual places. God likes to surprise us like that. I even found one in the aisle of a store while doing some shopping.

During a particularly challenging time in my life, several conch shells came across my pathway and I found encouragement in finding those as well. As I began to reflect on shells and various types, I asked God to reveal to me what He wanted me to share about the shells. I have concluded that the first shell I found may represent when we first come to Christ. We are small in size regarding our spiritual knowledge and we have much to learn, but no matter where we are, God can find us just as He allowed me to find the shell. As young believers, we have much to learn, but by following Christ, we will mature into something wonderful. The barnacle shell I once found reminds me of our lives when we get off the pathway of following God. We can become scarred and ugly like barnacles because of sin in our life causing us to hide and feel useless, but God's grace can change those ugly scars. I also found a shell underneath a hotel foundation one time which was protected by the elements. It was almost flawless, showing only a few marks, reminding me that our sins can be erased as we become protected under the shadow of God's wings.

As a young girl I use to put conch shells up to my ear to "hear the ocean." I was amazed at the sound and mesmerized by what I was hearing. A seashell surely reminds us of the importance of listening to God. Just as He led me to find the shells throughout my life, He wants to direct you too. Some of you may be hiding in your shells and not sharing your gifts and talents that would help to further His kingdom. Maybe you feel all washed up and no longer useful. I remind you that God can use you no matter where you are or whatever your age. He has a plan for your life and it is not over until your last breath.

I once received a sympathy card that had the picture of a seashell on the front and the following words "seashells remind us that every passing life leaves something beautiful behind." I encourage you to listen to God, come out of your shell and work towards leaving something beautiful behind.

"The sea belongs to Him, for He made it. His hands formed the dry land, too. Come, let us worship and bow down. Let us kneel before the Lord our maker, for He is our God. We are the people He watches over, the flock under His care. If only you would listen to His voice today! (Psalm 95:5–7, NLT)

Ponder this:

Can you recognize His voice? What is God speaking to you today?

Place a seashell in close view to remind you of the importance of listening to God or explore your own lesson from a shell.

Day 40
Life Rafts

Casually I watched a little group of girls the other day splashing around in the pool. As I shivered in my lounge chair, I admired both their energy and willingness to get into a pool of water when it was 60 degrees outside! They enthusiastically went about their morning, laughing, splashing and enjoying the day. One little girl made a game out of rounding up all the rafts for the lazy river which was connected to the pool. She seemed intent on keeping them all together. Her actions got me to thinking about the possibilities for this little girl and how she will most likely go into a field of caring for others one day. It was just the way she presented herself and her frantic desire to round up all the rafts and keep them together. I feel that way about my family sometimes, especially as I grow older. I just want to round up all of us and stay together. Knowing that we have each other gives my heart great comfort. God of course is our Father and He provides all things, but I feel He has given us family and friends to help provide a purpose and to help us remain grounded, focusing on others instead of ourselves.

Family and friends are in essence like life rafts. Provided the relationships are healthy and not torn apart, both can be a source of unity and love that is incomparable. Today, be grateful for all the caregivers in your life such as teachers and mentors who have helped to save you along life's journey. Don't be afraid to throw out your life raft to others along the way. You just might be saving a life for eternity.

**"This is good and pleases God our Savior,
who wants everyone to be saved
and to understand the truth."
(1 Timothy 2:3–4, NLT)**

Ponder this:

Are you quick to share the love of Christ with others?

Do you know someone who needs Christ? Commit to pray daily for this person. Perhaps you are the one to lead them to Christ.

Day 41
Mission Field

Sometimes I think I would like to go on a mission trip. Not sure if I am up to overseas travels or even if I'm really that adventurous. And it would sure be a true test for me considering my anxieties about flying at times. But the desire is there nonetheless. I am just curious if I have what it takes to do it. Do you ever have that thought of "do I have what it takes?"

There is something freeing about packing up the tee-shirts, jeans, tennis shoes, and ball caps and leaving behind all the other stuff like jewelry, pretty shoes, fancy clothes, etc. and just being available to others. Mission fields are everywhere though. We aren't all called overseas, but we are called. Called every day to be examples of Christ. Called every day to smile, encourage, engage, and uplift others.

Somedays, perhaps we ourselves are the mission field. We are the ones who need uplifting and encouraging, so we must keep our eyes, ears, and hearts open to that as well. God will encourage you! God will also give plenty of opportunities to go and do for others. Your field might just be out your back door, standing in line at the grocery store or seeing a neighbor who needs your smile. Don't miss the assignment. Keep your eyes open!

"He said to his disciples,
"The harvest if great, but the workers are few.
So, pray to the Lord who is in charge of the harvest;
ask Him to send more workers into his fields."
(Matthew 9:37–38, NLT)

Ponder this:

Where are you being called to be a mission field at this time in your life?

Do you truly understand that God needs you to witness to others about His love? When was the last time you did so?

Day 42
Passion

I have fond memories of my Mamaw always giving time and money to Missions through the Baptist Church. She was so active in her WMU (Women's Mission Union). I never knew what she actually did but I know she was passionate and consistent in her involvement. I remember her going to lots of meetings on Wednesday evenings; such dedication! I wish I could be the age I am now and have her back so I could ask her questions about her passions. Did she always have passion, or did she find it later in life?

As far as I know, Mamaw never wavered from her passion or support of missions. I can see her now adjourning from the prayer meetings with her Bible in hand making her way back into the congregational pew. It is a powerful image and I thank God for the memory and I thank my Mamaw too, for her devotion to God's mission field.

As long as God is part of your life, know that your passion will follow suit. My Mamaw's passion and purpose in life did not go unnoticed by the younger me at the time or by the older me of today. May it be so with you as well. Remember, others are watching, so be an example of Christ.

"This is what the Lord says – your Redeemer,
the Holy One of Israel: "I am the Lord your God,
who teaches you what is good for you
and leads you along the paths you should follow."
(Isaiah 48:17, NLT)

Ponder this:

Ask God today to show you your true passion in life if you don't already know.

How can you better develop your passion?

Day 43
The Favor of God

My Papaw…what a gem of a man he was! He was an encourager too! I have wonderful memories of him always laughing and displaying a quiet demeanor as well. He encouraged me to sing; always inviting me and my brother up to sing on Sunday evenings. I would rehearse from the hymnal on Sunday afternoons for a song he would direct on Sunday evenings. He would smile as I picked out the notes on the piano. Sometimes I would fake my way thru on the organ but mostly another little girl got to play the organ because she really was better. No matter, Papaw had a way of making me feel relaxed and okay when I most needed it. He was there when my parents divorced; providing shelter, food, and encouragement to Mom and us kids. What a wonderful legacy of a Godly man he left behind as well as mighty fine children and grandchildren.

I believe that because Papaw and Mamaw were followers of Christ that we, as their off-spring, have the favor of God upon us as long as we follow Him. I believe this to be true for all followers of Christ and their generations as well. It does not mean that life will always be smooth or easy, but it does mean that our Heavenly Father will reward the obedience of His followers. Like most people, my Papaw had a life before Christ, but he was redeemed and changed and went on to be a wonderful example of God's chosen men.

Know that the hand of God is on your life too. Even those who are beginning a new generation have the favor of God with them. We are redeemed, changed, and sanctified to become a living testimony of God's grace and favor.

"Soon the world will no longer see me, but you will see me.
Since I live, you also will live. When I am raised to life again,
you will know that I am in my Father,
and you are in me, and I am in you.
Those who accept my commandments
and obey them are the ones who love me.
And because they love me, my Father will love them.
And I will love them and reveal myself to each of them."
(John 14:19–21, NLT)

Ponder this:

Where in your life do you see the favor of God?

Who in your family is a living example of Christ? Pray for and be thankful for this individual or individuals right now.

Day 44

Sweeping

Nothing brings satisfaction to me like sweeping the floor. I mean, so much gets accomplished at one time! You get the benefit of a clean floor in addition to there being a great time to think and sort out things in the brain and talk to God. I see it as a great coping strength for multi-tasking and dealing with life issues. Sweeping has always been a great stress reducer for me. When I'm frustrated, anxious, stressed, mad, or just trying to figure things out in my head…I sweep! But I also talk out-loud to God during this time. With my broom just a'goin across the dusty floor and my thoughts flying out of my mouth I get a lot accomplished. I think it is a heathy way to cope with life's challenges and to tell you the truth, I have been doing it throughout my lifetime.

As a child, I grew up in an anxious home setting. There were arguments and fights between my parents and I would always reach for a broom and start sweeping to help calm my feelings. My younger siblings joked about me always having a broom in my hand and they called me the "Wicked Witch" who always rode her broom. I hope I was not wicked but I took their joke in fun and we still laugh about it to this day.

Jesus doesn't care where we talk to Him. He is ultimately the one who brings peace and calm to our lives. Having healthy means of coping is wonderful and we all need that, but nothing can replace the peace of Jesus. He is capable of accomplishing anything and no task is too great! Don't sweep all your cares under a rug, just give them to Jesus who cares about every detail of your life.

**"And the very hairs on your head are all numbered.
So, don't be afraid; you are more valuable to God
than a whole flock of sparrows."
(Luke 12:7, NLT)**

Ponder this:

How do you cope with feelings of stress and anxiety?

Are your ways of coping healthy?

Write your anxious thoughts in a journal. It is a great stress releasor and very therapeutic. Giving the mind a break by writing is good for the soul; it resembles praying somewhat. Something good just might come out of it, like a book!

Day 45
Labels

Labels are a big pet peeve with me. I dislike going to a store and buying something nice to display and then having to peel off the labels before I'm able to use or enjoy. Ever notice how the labels are never in a good place? You have to scrape and scrape to remove them and to me they are so ugly to look at; I even remove the price stickers from bread packages, but that might be a little much!

Labels on people are not good either. You stick or label someone with a name, an untruth or anything good or bad, and it could damage a person forever. We all get labeled in some form throughout our lives with sticky untruths about how others might perceive us. We must remember who we are in Christ and not rely on labels to identify us. We have various characteristics that make us unique, but some hurtful labels have been placed on us since childhood and it is time we outgrow or remove the labels that have marked us.

By knowing who you are in Christ, you can better let the labels of your past become unglued. You might have to work hard to remove them, but anything is possible through Christ our Savior so let Him do the job of removing labels that might be stuck in your memory. Imagine them being peeled and washed away by our Savior. Remember, no job is too hard for Him who loves you and there is only one label you should be wearing: A Child of the Highest God.

"For you are all children of God through faith in Christ Jesus."
(Galatians 3:26, NLT)

Ponder this:

Are you still wearing hurtful labels from your past?

Ask God to forgive the person who labeled you. Claim this day that you are a child of the Highest God!

Day 46
Courage

I'm seated next to a first-time flyer. She commented how small the windows are as she sat down. Very cute and nervous. I remember my first flight, so perhaps I can be a comfort to her. In my pious thoughts I perceived her as the weaker one which makes me feel stronger. Strange way to think and I am not sure if it's right but my goal is to help possibly make her trip more relaxed.

There is no one seated to her left; she occupies the middle seat so I began to explain take-off and the various loud noises she might hear throughout the trip. She commented that my voice was relaxing and I offered to have her sit by the window but she was content with just casually looking over my shoulder to take a peek out. She spoke about her kids and how proud they would be of her accomplishing this adventure and we shared other chit-chat kind of stuff.

Funny, that morning before I left home, I went to my bowl of inspirational rocks and shells and withdrew a stone with the word "courage" inscribed into it. I don't like to fly but I know that God speaks to me most when I face my fears. I have written many devotions while on a plane so facing my fears has allowed me to be with God during times of uncertainty. I chose the stone for my own benefit that morning, but as we exited the plane, I reached into my purse and gave it to the girl seated next to me. I said, "Here, this is meant for you today for you sure did show lots of courage." She got tears in her eyes and said "You helped to give me peace and it was God who put me beside you today." I like to think so too.

Trust that wherever you are today, is where you will find God waiting to give you your assignment and He will provide all the courage you need.

**"For He will order His angels to protect you wherever you go.
They will hold you up with their hands
so you won't even hurt your foot on a stone."
(Psalm 91:11–12, NLT)**

Ponder this:

Purchase or make your own inspirational rocks that can be shared with others. Keep one for yourself that reminds you of being courageous in Christ.

Day 47
It Is What It Is

Sometimes in life we are given a perfectly beautiful day. All is going well, sailing along smoothly, and yet we hesitate to embrace what is…right now…in the moment. It is as if we are afraid to trust all that is perfect for fear of cursing it.

Take for example my being 30,000 feet in the air right now. The flight is smooth, the weather beautiful, and I'm relaxing by writing in my journal. But my mind wants to wander into the "what if's" instead of "what is." What is…right now…is close to perfect. I can sit back and relax or choose to worry about potential bad weather, catching a cold from someone else, the plane going down, or being late so that I miss the next flight.

The what ifs of life can and will produce anxiety and can rob us of the joy God has in the moment. It is important to hold the what ifs captive so that the perfect moments can be enjoyed to the fullest. After all, this moment is all we have. All that is perfect is from God and is meant for your enjoyment so try not to complicate life by letting your thoughts run wild. If your thoughts get ahead of you, ask God to bring you back to the moment of peaceful and relaxing thoughts. Reflect on His goodness and know that He knows all about what is at this given moment in your life. Thanks be to God for all things!

"Thank God for this gift too wonderful for words!"
(2 Corinthians 9:15, NLT)

Ponder this:

Do you hesitate to enjoy life to the fullest for fear of letting your guard down and worrying about something bad happening?

How can you take your thoughts captive this day?

Day 48
The Eagle

I first noticed the fantastic creation while having lunch near a large window overlooking water and a mound of grass. The clouds were large and puffy and I spotted the eagle close enough to see its large white head and white tail. My view of this majestic being was so perfect that I actually saw the feathered formation of its tail from underneath while it soared above. And soar it did. I watched in utter amazement as the eagle kept climbing with such ease, higher and higher into the clouds until it became almost a small black dot. I watched as it rose upward and upward without even having to flap its wings. The wind carried it. And isn't that just what God does for us?

Life isn't about how far or high God will take us, but how much we trust Him to get us there. Just as the eagle trusts the wind, we too must trust God to carry us to new adventures and heights. It will not always be smooth. There will be wind, turbulence, unforeseen and unpredictable events, but we must trust! The eagle trusts the wind will always be there, and we too must know this about God. Just like the eagle, we can soar easily at times as God lifts our wings, but then too, we might also have to do a little flapping ourselves. Trust that God will always be beneath, around, and above you wherever you may go. Don't be afraid of new heights and adventures!

"But those who trust in the Lord will find new strength.
They will soar high on wings like eagles.
They will run and not grow weary.
They will walk and not faint."
(Isaiah 40:31, NLT)

Ponder this:

Do you feel like you are flapping your wings extra hard these days to stay in flight?

How can you know that God wants you to rest in the shelter of His wings? Where do you feel He is taking you?

Day 49
Material Gain

I am at a time in my life where I am examining that which I have accumulated and it is a lot! A lot of unnecessary stuff to say the least. There was a time when I was younger that I could shop 'til I dropped with the best of them. I still enjoy shopping but I have noticed that I gravitate to the smaller shops where my choices are limited and I don't feel as overwhelmed by so many of this and that's.

One day I felt in my heart the following: do not begrudge not going to the mall, not shopping; instead, rejoice regarding this time of self-reflection and examine closely whatever it is you are doing in service for Him, for the eternal rewards far outweigh the material gain. I believe God wants us to enjoy nice things, but we should not let shopping or any other distraction take away from our time with God.

Learn how to fill up on Him through prayer, Bible study, and fellowship with other believers. Whatever it is that you enjoy, make God a part of it. Be bold to ask Him for bargains and most importantly to control your finances and giving. Giving to others is never a mistake and can be beneficial in so many ways to ourselves and others. Remember to be a good steward of all that you have and that includes your time with God.

**"Be not deceived; God is not mocked:
for whatsoever a man soweth,
that shall he also reap."
(Galatians 6:7, KJV)**

Ponder this: Are you at a time in your life where you are done accumulating?

What might be interfering with your quiet time with God? What will you do to change this?

Day 50
Nothing Came

I was waiting on God one morning to give me another devotion to write…you know, waiting on inspiration. I assured myself that I was in the right place and time and frame of mind regarding my writing. Still nothing came. Nothing except this title: Nothing Came. I'm like, how can I write a devotion on that? But you know, sometimes we feel that way; just ho-hum, just low-key and thinking, is this all there is to life? Accumulating stuff, spending money, filling life with work, family and friends. and just plugging along; not challenging ourselves, staying stuck, being lazy in our witness for God. Is this it?

Realizing I was being very negative in my thoughts, my mind began to work towards bettering my mood. I wondered, what if we flipped a switch in our minds, reprogramed ourselves, re-charged, unplugged, and changed our surrounding a bit? I'm not talking about drastic changes, just subtle ones like learning a new hobby, exploring a trail, unplugging from technology, trying a new food, etc. When we become too comfortable and mundane in life, we can experience feelings of boredom and negativity.

Look for new ways to explore God's world, get outside your box and experience all that God has waiting for you. We should look for God in all things and perhaps then we will not feel as if nothing came along in our day. Strive this day to make something out of nothing and ask God to open your eyes to all His marvelous ways.

**"The precepts of the Lord are right, giving joy to the heart.
The commands of the Lord are radiant giving light to the eyes."
(Psalm 19:7, KJV)**

Ponder this:

Do you need to flip a switch in your mind regarding negative mindset?

Unplug from technology for half an hour this day and devote the time to God. What is He speaking to your spirit?

Day 51
Our Hero

Wanting to hear from God and waiting on Him can be difficult sometimes. Ofttimes it may seem as if nothing is happening in our lives, but we have to remember that sometimes God is fighting a battle for us that we know nothing about. It is a battle between good and evil. His delays are always on purpose and He is always fighting on our behalf so never think that He has forgotten you.

Think of God as a superhero just waiting in the nick of time to swoop down on your behalf and rescue you from harm. In the meantime, use common sense regarding life and worry and put your armor on. It is biblical to do so and if God has instructed us to do it, then we better heed His advice knowing there must be a good reason. God will arrive at just the right moment. You are too important for Him to give up on. Be assured that He is fighting your battles and He has already won. As scripture says, "For our struggle is not against flesh and blood, but against the rulers, against the authorities, against the powers of this dark world and against the spiritual forces of evil in the heavenly realms" (Ephesians 6:12, NIV).

We have nothing to fear for our God is the superhero who is only a call away.

**"Therefore, take up the full armor of God,
that you may be able to resist in the evil day,
and having done everything, to stand firm."
(Ephesians 6:13, NASB)**

Ponder this:

Read Ephesians 6:14–17 to learn more about the armor of God.

God is not a fake superhero; He is alive and real so trust that He will rescue you. Give Him all your concerns this day. Ask God to rescue you from anything He deems harmful in your life.

Day 52
What Competes with Your Attention?

It is so easy to get distracted in life. So much going on at all times. It takes discipline to stay in the moment. Focusing on the here and now is a newly coined phrase in society; I'm not sure who came up with that. The mind can only process so many things at one time.

We as a society are told to multitask, to keep up, to do more...but (there is always a but where God is concerned) God teaches us the importance of listening to the Holy Spirit and how will we ever hear His voice, His guidance if we are constantly moving and challenging ourselves to do more and be more?

I challenge you today (remember, you are not reading this devotion by happenchance) to relax, rest, be quiet, and not give in to the guilt of being more than you are at this moment. God's love is unconditional. If we are truly devoted to God and follow His commandments, we will want to do what is right and good in life. He does not love us more when we do more. He does not love us less when we do less. He loves us because we are His children and that my friend...is enough.

"My child, never forget the things I have taught you.
Store my commands in your heart.
If you do this, you will live many years
and your life will be satisfying."
(Proverbs 3:1–2, NLT)

Ponder this:

Do you find yourself easily distracted regarding the tasks at hand?

How can you better stay on track to accomplish what God wants you to do?

Can you take some time today to just rest and relax and give yourself permission to just be?

Day 53
Lessons from a Stray Dog

Two years ago, my husband and I adopted a rescue dog which had been found as a stray roaming the streets of South Carolina. I think he dropped into our laps straight from heaven for he was housebroken and had such a calm spirit. God must have known now that I am a bit older, I would not have the energy to train a puppy. I have had the pleasure of teaching him a few tricks and one day as I was commanding him to sit and stay, it occurred to me that our God would like nothing better sometimes than for us to both sit and stay.

Sitting for a while, just listening to His voice and staying with Him in thanksgiving has such wonderful rewards. Just as I reward my doggie with a treat for good behavior, God will reward us with a peaceful spirit and wisdom far beyond measure, but we must first be disciplined to come, sit, and stay in His presence.

**"And he said, how can I, except some man should guide me?
And he desired Philip that he would come up and sit with Him."
(Acts 8:31, KJV)**

Ponder this:

Spend some time just sitting before God. Have no expectations, just sit with Him for a while.

If it is hard for you to sit, challenge yourself to just 5 minutes at a time. If your mind wants to wander, just calmly ask God to help you remain focused on Him.

Day 5 4
The Holy Spirit

We can get ourselves in a whole mess of trouble when we do not listen to the Holy Spirit. I know firsthand the side effects of disobeying or ignoring His promptings. It isn't intentional, but sometimes as humans we run with our own agendas.

For example, today I wanted to go and look at a furniture store for a possible new sofa. I spent much time picking out my clothes, doing my hair and makeup and I bounced down the steps preparing for my adventure of sofa searching. Just as I hit the bottom step a feeling came over me (guilt probably) that caused me to stop, and a thought came to me that I should write instead. My head wanted to justify that it was Saturday and okay for me to go out and enjoy myself. A feeling came to my spirit that said, you can go out later but for now, you need to write. "But God, I have nothing to write about," I reasoned. "Go and sit down at your computer and trust me," He prompted. So here I sit, typing this message to you the reader.

When God prompts you…listen. It will truly be for your benefit and possibly someone else's too. Try not to be in such a hurry each day that you fail to ask God, "What would you have me do today?" Right now, I still have sofa searching on my mind but God understands human desires. He will give us the desires of our hearts when we are obedient to His will. Call upon the Holy Spirit for He will give you all the direction you need for your day!

I did eventually find the perfect sofa…in God's time and it was worth waiting for.

**"Call unto me, and I will answer thee,
and show thee great and mighty things,
which thou knowest not."
(Jeremiah 33:3, KJV)**

Ponder this:

Do you allow the Holy Spirit to direct you on a regular basis? How much better could your life be by allowing this?

As a follower of Christ, you have the power of the Holy Spirit within you. If you do not know Christ, call a Pastor to help you in making this decision. All you have to do is believe and invite Christ into your life.

Day 55

When Flood Waters Come

There is a big storm brewing out in the Atlantic Ocean right now. It is headed right towards North Carolina and I watch with sadness in my heart for the devastation it has caused so far. Flood waters can rush in and destroy in a minute what took years to build.

Thankfully, God is a restorer of all things, but it takes time and ofttimes things are restored to even better than they were before. When tragedy hits, it puts things into perspective, sometimes causing us to examine the truly important things in life and appreciating the blessings. Flood waters can come in various forms in our lives; not just raging waters but other incidents that seem to overtake us and cause us to fear and fret. Be assured, God is in control and He knows just when we need rescuing from situations that He deems harmful to us.

We don't have the capacity to always see what is ahead for us in life, but we need to trust God that if we make a bad decision or a wrong turn, He will put us back on track and step in to protect us from drowning in life's storms.

> "'My thoughts are nothing like your thoughts', says the Lord.
> 'And my ways are far beyond anything you could imagine.
> For just as the heavens are higher than the earth,
> so my ways are higher than your ways
> and my thoughts higher than your thoughts.'"
> (Isaiah 55:8–9, NLT)

Ponder this:

What do you do when it seems as if the flood waters of life are raging all around you?

Ask God this day to protect you with His army of warriors and trust that He cares for you! Call a friend and share your concerns asking for prayer if the situation feels difficult.

Day 56
Chirping Along

I was applying my makeup when a bright red cardinal appeared outside my window. Cardinals, as I've said before, have always served as an inspiration to me, so I paused and watched as he climbed to various limbs and heights on the branches of the holly tree. So vivid was his color that I sat in amazement and quietly listened to his chirp-chirp song.

I believe we too are chirping to our own beat and purpose in life, for we are all uniquely designed by our Holy Creator. It's wonderful to know our gifts and talents can be used for God's glory. This day however, you may be thinking, "I have no purpose." But I want to encourage you to think of all the people you come in contact with on a weekly basis. Do you know your smile, laugh, pat on the back, and encouraging words can and could make all the difference in another person's life and could impact eternity? Sometimes we are the ones who need the encouragement, but never discount the potential you have to impact the life of another person. We are all messengers of God and He relies on us to help spread His word based on various experiences in our lives where we have seen Him at work. Your own life experiences may very well help to encourage someone else who might be experiencing the same life event.

Just like the cardinal, be willing to share the unique chirp God has placed in your heart. Pay attention to the people, nature, and events that God sends your way today, and may your song be a joyous one!

**"If your gift is to encourage others, be encouraging.
If it is giving, give generously.
If God has given you leadership ability,
take the responsibility seriously.
And if you have a gift for showing kindness to others,
do it gladly."
(Romans 12:8, NLT)**

Ponder this:

Make a list of the qualities God has given you. Are you using your qualities to help others?

Day 57
In the Palm of His Hand

I sing in the choir with a lady who is a bit of a mentor to me. We were rehearsing before Sunday service and she really liked the words to one of the songs that reminded us that God holds us in the palm of His hand.

I used to visualize when I was flying during turbulence that God had the whole plane in the palm of His hand. His feet were firmly planted on the ground and He had me encased tightly and securely! It is true for you too. Even if life feels out of control, crazy, and overwhelming at times…God has us! There is nothing we feel that Jesus Himself did not experience. He understands.

For just a moment right now, pause, and imagine Him holding you. Breathe. Take in all His presence and goodness. Trust that God has you right where you are intended to be this day. Through the turbulent times, the smooth times, and the uncertain times, God has you in the palm of His hand. I can think of no better place to be, can you?

**"For I the Lord thy God will hold thy right hand,
saying unto thee, Fear not; I will help thee."
(Isaiah 41:13, KJV)**

Ponder this:

When have you felt the hand of God carrying you?

Have you shared this experience of God carrying you with others?

If not, make it a priority to do so, for others can benefit by the sharing of your story.

Day 58
As the Deer
Pants for the Water

The deer in my woods love to quench their thirst by drinking from the backyard bird bath. It warms my heart to see them there at various times throughout the day, more so in the summer.

One day as I was lugging water in a container to pour into the birdbath, I was reminded of a Scripture verse; "As a deer pants for the water, so my soul cries out to thee," at least that is how I remembered the verse. Do we have a true thirst for God? Are we seeking to find it through stories in the Bible, searching the Scripture for His advice, listening to His guidance by the Holy Spirit? I know for me personally I find His presence through the observance of nature and God's creations. I truly do not know what I would do without my Bible and God's encouraging words and being able to take in nature. The older I get, the more I want to soak up His word which quenches all that ails me. I think of that Scripture verse every time I provide water for the deer.

God provides everlasting water of abundance to each of us. He quenches our thirsts and heart desires throughout all of our lifetime. Eternity awaits all believers and life there will be unlike anything we have ever experienced. Until then, all we have to do is drink from that which He has provided…just like the deer.

**"As the deer longs for streams of water, so I long for you,
Oh God. I thirst for God, the living God.
When can I go and stand before Him?"
(Psalm 42:1–2, NLT)**

Ponder this:

What encouragement do you glean from nature?

Do you feel God is providing all your needs? If not, continue to ask Him to guide your desires and to be in agreement with Him.

Day 59

Rest

Battling a cold will cause the body to demand that it be rested. We hurry about so in life doing important things but also things that do not amount to much in the long run. The body was not designed to go full speed all the time and we are badly mistaken if we think we can run full speed ahead throughout our lives. We are not invincible, we will wear out, so that is why it is important to slow down and listen to our body.

Often, if we listen close enough, we will feel the prompting of the Holy Spirit to rest prior to getting a cold or worse. Coming to a screeching halt in life is no fun. How many times in our lives have we been interrupted with an illness and we think, I do not have time for this! But aren't you ever so slightly grateful for the pause, the break, the day in bed to just be? If you are perfectly honest with yourself, the answer will be, yes! God designed us to only be able to handle so much at one time and sometimes in our urgency to get it all done, we burn out, drain ourselves, get sick, and become depleted.

Learn to recognize when your body is speaking to you. Do not feel guilty for resting, regrouping, refocusing, or just relaxing. Remember, we were created in the image of God and He designed us to rest and enjoy all He has created in a spirit of peace.

**"It is useless for you to work so hard
from early morning until late at night,
anxiously working for food to eat;
for God gives rest to His loved ones."
(Psalm 127:2, NLT)**

Ponder this:

When was the last time you were able to have a day of true rest? Can you ask a friend to help out in order for you to do so?

Even Jesus rested, so it must be important for us as well. Can you rest without feeling guilty? What would a day of rest look like for you?

Day 60
Leap of Faith

Sitting quietly in my living room listening to the wind howling outside, I notice a little crocheted frog sticker on my glass that I had been sipping tea from all day. The frog is posed as if he is getting ready to leap somewhere. Frogs were designed to leap; it is part of their nature. Noticing the frog with his long legs stretched out got me to thinking about my own life and those times when I have taken a leap of faith or failed to. I do not relish flying, but I have gotten on many airplanes and times I felt most anxious were leaps of faith for me. Going back to school and getting my bachelor and masters degree were huge leaps of faith. At this time in my life, writing a book is a huge leap of faith.

God puts desires in our hearts and at times we want to jump at chances offered to us. I know at times I can almost feel ready to leap and then I get scared and bombard my mind with thoughts of "what if this or what if that?" But God has blessed me with many God Moments because of my obedience in trusting Him. There would have been many missed blessings if I had not listened to the prompting of the Holy Spirit. But I did miss opportunities, times I did not leap due to fear or lack of confidence.

Sometimes we do not know if an opportunity is from God or our own desires. This is a time when we really need to pause and listen, and seek Godly counsel from a trusted friend, mentor or pastor if necessary. God will reveal His will for you and will bless your endeavors. Begin today to trust, pray, and leap when necessary.

**"For I know the plans I have for you declares the Lord,
plans to prosper you and not to harm you,
plans to give you hope and a future."
(Jeremiah 29:11, NLT)**

Ponder this:

What leap of faith is God asking you to take?

Set some goals regarding areas where you feel God is asking you to trust Him.

Day 61

A Magic Wand

Someone once challenged me with this question, "If you could wave a magic wand, what would you do with it?" I never hesitated and said that I would become a counselor. It took me twenty years to fulfill that desire, and at the time, it really was an impulsive response to the question. But somehow, I believe I was speaking from the heart that day.

Sometimes we do not know what the heart wants. We tend to do and become based on what society demands of us and we wear many hats and complete many great things but how many of us are truly following our hearts, and what does that really mean?

God plants seeds of desire inside each of us based on the gifts and talents He has so generously bestowed upon us. Sometimes we learn we have hidden talents we never knew we had and will only be discovered as we take one step of faith after another. These steps are leading to hidden gems in our lives; things we would never imagine possible. Life with Jesus can be exciting and rewarding. He reveals so much about Himself as we walk hand in hand with Him and He truly does want to give us the desires of our hearts even when we do not know what that might be.

What would waving a magic wand look like for you? What would change if Jesus were holding the wand instead of you; ever consider that? There is nothing magic about God but living for Him can truly feel magical...that is how good He truly is.

**"And whatsoever ye do, do it heartily
as to the Lord and not unto men."
(Colossians 3:23, KJV)**

Ponder this:

If you could be or do anything, what would that be?

Do you feel that God has placed desires in your heart that He wants to accomplish in your life?

Who holds the magic wand…you, or Jesus?

Day 62

Live for Eternity

I was getting ready to turn the final copy of this book in to the publisher. Everything was finished and I was at peace, or so I thought. I had 61 devotions and that is the age I am as I am writing this book. That is perfect I told myself. However, God spoke to my heart to end this devotional book with a reminder to the readers to live their earthly life with an eternal perspective. I thought about a conversation I had with my mother one day about not having anything to look forward to. Mom was sick with lung cancer and my heart broke with the likelihood of losing her. We got to taking about what heaven might be like and I told mom, "you have heaven to look forward to." She smiled and said, "yes, I sure do!"

Living with an eternal perspective helps to lessen the pain of earthly life sometimes. My heart misses my mom so very much and the only solace I have is knowing I will see her again someday, in Heaven. Heaven, a place our minds cannot even begin to comprehend. There has got to be unending beauty there. The Bible paints a beautiful picture and those words alone are enough to give us hope.

Hope is what we all need right now. In a world that has gotten so off course and reckless in so many ways. Maybe you have become a bit reckless too. We all do. But God is there to put us back on track. Sometimes I think it would do us all some good to spend time thinking about eternity. None of us like to think about dying, but it will happen. Heaven is the final resting place for believers.

I like to imagine my Mom up there playing the piano on the grandest piano ever designed. She probably sits quietly with Jesus by a river talking and has picnics with her loved ones. I know my mind can't begin to behold all we will see, but I think Jesus doesn't mind if we dream a little bit about what it might be like. Thinking of eternity might just help us get through the earthly trials a little bit better.

So now I end with 62 devotions. Perfect, for that is the age I will be when this book is printed! Thanks be to God for His fingerprints on my life, on your life, and the wonderful eternal place called Heaven where we will bow at His feet.

**"The twelve gates were twelve pearls:
each individual gate was of one pearl.
And the street of the city was pure gold,
like transparent glass."
(Revelation 21:21, NKJV)**

Ponder this:

What is your picture of heaven?

Who are you looking most forward to seeing in heaven?

If you were to die today, are you ready to see Jesus?

God invites all to come to believe in Him. If you do not have a personal relationship with Jesus, just say a simple prayer and invite him into your life. Tell someone today of your decision. God welcomes you into His eternal family.

CPSIA information can be obtained
at www.ICGtesting.com
Printed in the USA
LVHW011131200222
711571LV00003B/48